EXPANSION OF OUR NATION

THE TEXAS REVOLUTION

by Xina M. Uhl

FOCUS READERS

FOCUS READERS

WWW.FOCUSREADERS.COM

Focus Readers is distributed by North Star Editions:
sales@northstareditions.com | 888-417-0195

Produced for Focus Readers by Red Line Editorial.

Content Consultant: Dr. Gideon Mailer, Associate Professor of History, University of Minnesota Duluth

Photographs ©: Everett Historical/Shutterstock Images, cover, 1, 10–11, 21; Daniel Powers Whiting/G. & W. Endicott/Library of Congress, 4–5; Red Line Editorial, 6, 25; Carol M. Highsmith/Carol M. Highsmith Archive/Library of Congress, 9, 22–23; Sean Pavone/Shutterstock Images, 13; Sipley/ClassicStock/Alamy, 14; Everett Collection/Newscom, 16–17; Christian Hinkle/Alamy, 18; North Wind Picture Archives, 27, 29

ISBN
978-1-63517-887-6 (hardcover)
978-1-63517-988-0 (paperback)
978-1-64185-191-6 (ebook pdf)
978-1-64185-090-2 (hosted ebook)

Library of Congress Control Number: 2018931700

Printed in the United States of America
Mankato, MN
May, 2018

ABOUT THE AUTHOR

Xina M. Uhl discovered her love of history while still in grade school. She went on to obtain a master of arts in history from California State University, Northridge. After teaching American history, she moved into educational writing. She has authored more than 20 books for young people.

TABLE OF CONTENTS

CHAPTER 1

TEXAS FACES CHANGES

In 1821, Mexico gained **independence** from Spain. By 1824, Mexico was a **republic** with 19 states and a few territories. One state in northeast Mexico was called Coahuila and Texas. This state was far away from the nation's capital, Mexico City. And there were not many roads to get to the state.

In the 1820s, some US citizens traveled to settle in the northeast part of Mexico.

Several American Indian tribes lived in Coahuila and Texas. But few Mexican citizens lived there. Mexico's leaders wanted more people to live in the state. So, they allowed US citizens to settle there. The settlers became known as

NORTH AMERICA (LATE 1820s)

Texians. Many of them were eager to get cheap land.

By 1830, approximately 16,000 Texians lived in the state. But they did not follow all of Mexico's requirements. Most did not become Catholics. And few learned to speak Spanish, the language of Mexico. In addition, the Texians traded mostly with the United States, not Mexico. Arguments often broke out between the Texians and the Tejanos. The Tejanos were the Mexican citizens who had lived in the area for many years.

Mexico's leaders were concerned. They thought the Texians might try to make Texas independent from Mexico.

Mexico's leaders also worried the United States might try to take over Texas.

Antonio López de Santa Anna became Mexico's president in 1833. Within two years, he changed the country's form of government. He made the government's power much more **centralized**. Mexico's states no longer had as much power.

Texians did not want this type of government control. In addition, some Mexican lawmakers wanted to make slavery illegal. Many Texians were slaveholders. They did not want to give up their slaves.

The Mexican government grew even stronger in 1834 and 1835. Its leaders

The Battle of Gonzales broke out when Texians in the town of Gonzales refused to give up their cannon.

began to worry that the Texians would fight back. And some did. Led by William Travis, they captured the town of Anahuac on June 30, 1835. So, Santa Anna sent Mexican soldiers to Texas.

In the town of Gonzales, Mexican soldiers ordered the Texians to turn over their cannon. The Texians refused. A battle broke out, and the Texians won.

CHAPTER 2

THE ALAMO

In November 1835, Texian leaders met in San Felipe de Austin. They agreed to fight against Santa Anna's government. They hoped other people in Mexico would help them remove Santa Anna from power. In this way, states could get back more control. Texas might even become a separate state from Coahuila.

President Santa Anna was a famous general. He had helped fight to make Mexico independent.

In December 1835, a small group of Texians forced the Mexican army out of San Antonio. San Antonio was the largest and most important city in Texas. Santa Anna was furious when he heard about this defeat. He gathered approximately 7,000 soldiers and rode for the city.

The Texians in San Antonio prepared for an attack. They holed up in the Alamo. Spanish **missionaries** had lived and worked in this group of buildings in the early 1700s. By the end of the 1700s, many of the buildings were in ruins. But the chapel still stood. The Mexicans had used the chapel as a military base. Now, the Texians would, too.

Visitors today can still see the Alamo chapel that the Texians defended.

Sam Houston led the Texian army. He ordered the Texians to abandon the Alamo. He did not think they could defend it from Santa Anna's army. But 150 men refused to leave. Jim Bowie and William Travis led this group. Davy Crockett also helped defend the Alamo.

Davy Crockett (holding knife) was a frontier hero who had come from the United States to help the Texians fight.

Santa Anna's army arrived on February 23, 1836. They laid siege to the Alamo. In this kind of attack, soldiers surround a town or building. The Mexican army greatly outnumbered the Texians. Travis tried to get more soldiers. He sent letters asking people to come and help fight. But only 32 men got past the Mexican forces and joined the Texians.

Even so, the Texians defended the Alamo for 13 days. They shot their guns and fired their cannons. Then ammunition began to run low. Travis knew they could not hold out much longer. Still, the men refused to give up.

On the morning of March 6, Mexican troops broke through the Alamo's walls. They charged into the mission. Two hours later, the fighting ended.

Mexico won the Battle of the Alamo, but at great cost. Hundreds of soldiers were killed or injured. Most of the Alamo's defenders died during the fighting. A few survivors were captured by the Mexican army. Santa Anna had them executed.

CHAPTER 3

THE BATTLES CONTINUE

Despite their defeat at the Alamo, the Texians did not give up. They cried, "Remember the Alamo!" They continued fighting for Texas to be independent from Mexico. A number of Texians had wanted this all along. After the Alamo, many more adopted this view. News of the fighting in Texas reached the southern United States.

Sam Houston was a key leader during Texas's fight for independence.

Texian leaders met at Washington-on-the-Brazos to make plans for a new government.

Many southerners traveled to Texas and joined the Texian army.

Meanwhile, Texian leaders had begun making plans for Texas to become a country. While the Alamo was under siege, Sam Houston met with other

delegates. They gathered in a place known as Washington-on-the-Brazos. On March 2, 1836, they issued the Texas Declaration of Independence. It stated that Texas was no longer a part of Mexico.

Next, the delegates worked to create a new government for Texas. Two weeks later, they adopted a constitution. This document was a guide for how the new country, known as the Republic of Texas, would be governed. However, Mexico's leaders did not accept these documents. They fought to keep control of Texas.

Several small battles took place at the town of Refugio between March 12 and March 15. The Mexican army won.

On March 19, a fight erupted at Coleto Creek. The Texians lost this battle, too. By the evening, the Mexican army had surrounded them. The Texians surrendered the next morning.

Mexican forces took the Texian soldiers prisoner. They held them captive at the nearby town of Goliad. Mexican general José de Urrea was in charge. He promised that the prisoners would not be harmed. However, Santa Anna told him to execute them. Urrea refused this order. But another Mexican officer, José Nicolás de la Portilla, carried it out.

On March 27, Portilla forced the Texian prisoners to march along nearby roads.

The Texian soldiers were held captive in the chapel of La Bahía Presidio in Goliad, Texas.

Mexican soldiers shot and killed 342 of the prisoners. Only 28 men escaped. This event became known as the Goliad Massacre. It made Texians very angry. Many US citizens were shocked, too. US support for the Texas **Revolution** grew.

CHAPTER 4

THE LAST BATTLE

Sam Houston continued gathering and training more soldiers. On April 21, 1836, he led approximately 900 men to the San Jacinto River. There, they made a surprise attack against the Mexican army.

The Battle of San Jacinto lasted for only 18 minutes. It was a great victory for the Texians. Only nine Texians were killed.

The Battle of San Jacinto was the final battle of the Texas Revolution.

However, 630 Mexican soldiers were killed. Also, Santa Anna was captured. The Texians forced him to sign a treaty. The treaty recognized the Republic of Texas as an independent country.

According to the Texians, the Texas Revolution ended when Santa Anna signed the treaty at San Jacinto. But Mexico disagreed. The Mexican government never ratified, or officially approved, the treaty. For this reason, Mexico argued that the treaty was invalid.

In addition, the two groups disagreed about Texas's borders. Texas insisted its southern border reached the Rio Grande. But Mexico said the border was at the

Nueces River. Mexico also objected to the western border Texas claimed.

People within the Republic of Texas were divided, too. People who had not supported the revolution could not be citizens. And they could not own property.

BATTLES OF THE TEXAS REVOLUTION

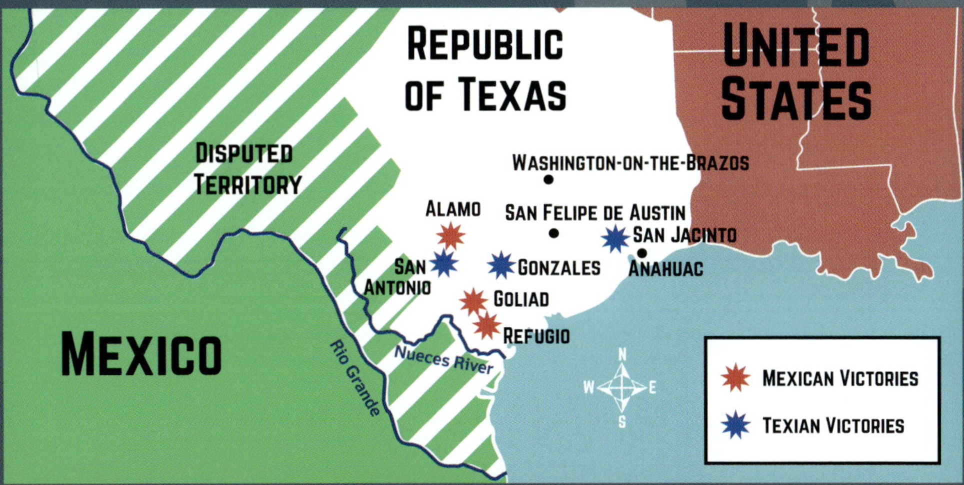

American Indians and black people could not be citizens either. Many Tejanos also faced **discrimination**, threats, or violence. As a result, many Tejanos fled to Mexico.

The Republic of Texas kept close ties with the United States. In fact, some Texians wanted to join the United States. They worried that Mexico would invade Texas. And they were not sure Texas was strong enough to defend itself. Plus, the new government struggled to get enough money. Becoming a US state seemed like a way to solve these problems.

In September 1836, the citizens of Texas voted for the United States to **annex** them. The US Congress had to

The Mexican–American War (1846–1848) began soon after Texas joined the United States.

approve this decision. Lawmakers argued for years about whether the new state would allow slavery. Texas finally became a state in December 1845. Mexico did not approve of this action. In April 1846, war broke out between the two nations. The Mexican–American War lasted until 1848. When it ended, Mexico agreed that Texas was part of the United States.

JUAN SEGUÍN

Juan Seguín was a Tejano resident of Texas. Like many Tejanos, Seguín opposed Santa Anna's government. He joined the Texians in fighting for Texas's independence. He also served as the mayor of San Antonio.

However, after the Texas Revolution, many towns chased Tejano residents away. Seguín was accused of being loyal to Mexico. Some Texians suspected him of treason. They chased him out of Texas. He was forced to return to Mexico.

Seguín felt betrayed by the people who did this. He called himself "a foreigner in my native land." Despite his efforts to see Texas "free and happy," he was separated from his home and family.

When Seguín got to Mexico, he was arrested. The Mexican government offered to release him if he joined the Mexican army. He agreed. Later,

Juan Seguín's family lived in San Antonio for many years. But after the Texas Revolution, he was forced to leave.

Seguín fought against the United States in the Mexican–American War.

FOCUS ON

THE TEXAS REVOLUTION

Write your answers on a separate piece of paper.

1. Write a paragraph that describes the main ideas of Chapter 1.

2. If you had lived in the Republic of Texas, would you have voted to join the United States? Why or why not?

3. Where did the last battle of the Texas Revolution take place?

A. San Antonio
B. Gonzales
C. San Jacinto

4. Why did the Republic of Texas have close ties with the United States?

A. Many people who lived in Texas had moved there from the United States.
B. Many people had moved from Texas to settle in the United States.
C. Both countries were led by the same president.

Answer key on page 32.

GLOSSARY

annex
To take over a country or territory.

centralized
Controlled by a single authority.

delegates
People who are selected to vote, act, or attend meetings on behalf of other people.

discrimination
Unfair treatment of others based on who they are or how they look.

independence
The ability to make decisions without being controlled by another government.

missionaries
People who teach religious beliefs and attempt to convince others of those beliefs.

republic
A country governed by elected leaders.

revolution
A complete change in a country's government, often a change that is sudden or violent.

TO LEARN MORE

BOOKS

Gunderson, Jessica. *The Alamo: Myths, Legends, and Facts*. North Mankato, MN: Capstone Press, 2015.

Micklos, John, Jr. *To the Last Man: The Battle of the Alamo.* North Mankato, MN: Capstone Press, 2016.

Walker, Paul Robert. *Remember the Alamo: Texians, Tejanos, and Mexicans Tell Their Stories*. Washington, DC: National Geographic, 2015.

NOTE TO EDUCATORS

Visit **www.focusreaders.com** to find lesson plans, activities, links, and other resources related to this title.

INDEX

Answer Key: 1. Answers will vary; **2.** Answers will vary; **3.** C; **4.** A